*First published in
the United States in 1991 by*
Gloucester Press
387 Park Avenue South
New York, NY 10016

Library of Congress Cataloging-in-Publication Data

Becklake, Sue
    Waste disposal and recycling / by Sue Becklake.
        p. cm. -- (Green Issues)
    Includes index.
    Summary: A look at such waste disposal problems as overflowing
landfills and hazardous waste and possible solutions for them, primarily
recycling.
    ISBN 0-531-17305-4
    1. Refuse and refuse disposal--Juvenile literature. 2. Recycling (Waste,
etc.)--Juvenile literature. [1. Refuse and refuse disposal. 2. Recycling
(Waste)] I. Title. II. Series.
TD792.B43 1991
363.72'8--dc20   91-9702   CIP   AC

Printed in Belgium

The publishers would like to acknowledge that
the photographs reproduced within this book
have been posed by models or have been
obtained from photographic agencies.

Design	David West
	Children's Book Design
Editor	Elise Bradbury
Picture research	Emma Krikler
Illustrator	Aziz Khan

*The author, Sue Becklake, has a degree in Science and has written
many books for children. This book was written in collaboration
with John Becklake.*

*The consultant, Brian Gardiner, is an atmospheric scientist. He
works for the British Antarctic Survey and was one of the three
scientists who discovered the hole in the ozone layer.*

WASTE DISPOSAL AND RECYCLING

SUE
BECKLAKE

GLOUCESTER PRESS
London · New York · Toronto · Sydney

CONTENTS

▷ The number of cars in the world is estimated to grow from 400 million today to 700 million in 20 years. All will end up as scrap metal. This does not have to be wasteful: scrap metal can be reprocessed into new metal products.

INTRODUCTION

Waste is anything we no longer want, from yesterday's newspaper to poisonous chemicals left over from industry. The amount of waste we produce is rising. This is partly because the world's population is growing fast. In addition, people buy more things, from clothes to televisions and cars, most of which end up as waste.

Waste does not disappear when we throw it away, it is just moved from one place to another. For centuries we have used the land to dump waste from our homes. We have piped wastes from factories into rivers and seas. Our industries and cars have released waste gases into the air. We now know that these wastes can poison wildlife and endanger human health. The industries and toxic waste dumps that surround the Great Lakes of North America have poisoned the water to such an extent that residents are warned it is not safe to eat fish from the lakes. In parts of Eastern Europe, pollution is so severe that people suffer chronic health problems.

Simply throwing things away when we are finished with them not only creates pollution, but is also wasteful of the earth's limited natural resources. Recycling and reusing materials is one alternative. Industry has been recycling materials like metals for some time, and projects are now being set up in local areas to recycle household garbage. A Swiss firm has developed a process that compacts domestic garbage into pellets which can be used as building materials. With this method, our food scraps, paper, and other garbage could be made into housing.

We can combat the urgent problem of waste if we employ the recycling methods that are being developed, and if we concentrate on producing less waste in the first place. However, if we refuse to recognize the problem, we will continue to poison our food, water, and air.

Chapter One

INCREASING WASTE

All living things produce waste. As life evolved, nature developed ways to reuse the waste from plants and animals. For example, small amounts of sewage can be consumed by bacteria and other living things. However, the world's five billion people now produce so much sewage that nature cannot cope with it all. Humans have also disrupted nature by developing a huge range of new chemicals like medicines and fertilizers, and materials like plastics, that do not rot naturally. These products have been vital in feeding us, clothing us, and making the goods we use every day. However, the manufacturing processes can cause pollution, and when we have finished with the products they become waste. This waste can then pollute the environment.

What is waste?

Usually we think of waste as the garbage that is thrown in the garbage can – cans, bottles, paper, and food scraps. An average European household throws out over 100 cans of garbage a year. But this is only a fraction of the total waste produced. At home, dirty water from sinks, baths, and washing machines disappears into the sewers with the waste we flush down the toilet. Our fires and central heating boilers burn gas, coal, or oil, releasing waste gases into the air. Gases also escape from the exhaust pipes of cars, trucks, and other kinds of transportation.

Industry and farming produce the vast majority of solid wastes, from animal manure from farming to waste rock from mining and scrap metal, and ash from factories. Small businesses, stores, and schools all produce waste as well. A few hundred years ago the amount of waste on earth was much smaller. There were fewer people, and their sewage was easily absorbed by the local rivers or sea. People

◁ Scarab beetles are one of nature's recyclers. They collect dung for food.

detergents, fertilizers, pesticides, and a host of others. Chemical fertilizers and pesticides have helped to more than double world food production since they started to be widely used 40 years ago.

Only a minority of chemicals in everyday use are potentially harmful. They are all ideal for specific purposes, but drawbacks may begin to appear after they have been in use for many years. For example, CFCs (chlorofluorocarbons) are extremely useful gases that are used in manufacturing some kinds of packaging and insulation, cleaning electronic circuits, and keeping refrigerators cool. They get into the atmosphere when they leak from broken-down refrigerators and air conditioners dumped on garbage dumps, or when factories that make these products release CFC gases.

Scientists have found that CFCs damage the ozone layer. This layer protects us from harmful ultraviolet radiation from the sun. Ultraviolet radiation is the main cause of skin cancer, a disease that kills 12,000 people a year in the United States. CFCs cause problems because they last for over 100 years, drifting into the atmosphere and releasing chlorine, which destroys ozone. They are now being phased out in many countries, but the CFCs already in the atmosphere will continue to damage the ozone layer for many years to come. The consequences could be severe.

We have introduced other materials to the environment that last for an extremely long time. Plastics are used in the manufacture of cars, domestic appliances, furniture, and clothing. Some plastics are even strong enough to be made into bullet-proof shields. Their strength and durability are an advantage until they are disposed of. Then they do not decompose like natural materials, but remain for hundreds of years

were not as quick to throw things away, so their garbage heaps were smaller. Many items were made of materials that rotted away naturally.

In the natural world, the waste produced by living things is recycled. Animal droppings and the bodies of dead animals and plants are broken down to provide food for other living things. The carbon dioxide and oxygen gases in the atmosphere are also constantly recycled. Carbon dioxide is absorbed by plants, which give out oxygen. Oxygen is necessary for animals and people to breathe. Throughout the 3.5 billion years that life forms have been developing, nature has become extremely efficient at dealing with waste.

New materials
The kind of waste we throw away has changed over the years. During the last 50 years, a huge range of materials have been developed that do not exist in nature. Many of these have proved extremely useful, including plastics, artificial fibers,

on the garbage dump. There are now some plastics that decompose when they are exposed to sunlight or buried in the soil. These have been used to make shampoo bottles in Germany and some plastic shopping bags. However, they are expensive and it is difficult to ensure that they will not decompose while in use.

The throwaway society

In the United States and other industrialized areas, like Western Europe, Australia, and Japan, people can buy a huge range of products. The populations in these regions have more money to spend, and this has changed people's attitudes to buying things. In the 1950s, factories manufactured goods with increasing speed and needed to sell them. To do this they had to persuade people to buy more. With the help of advertising they started a consumer boom, which means people were buying more than ever before.

The problem is that people also began throwing out more. Advertising persuaded us that where one product was used before, we now needed more than one, and that the latest product was an improvement on all the others. Although manufacturers can make vehicles that would last for decades, they build cars that wear out much sooner so they can sell more of them. As fashions change, we replace things before they wear out, buying a new version and throwing away the old one. In the past, most things were built to last and were valued for their durability. Now things are often valued for their cheapness, and are thrown away and replaced far more often.

Another change has occurred in the way we shop. Everything is wrapped individually so that we can take the goods from the shelves ourselves. When we have paid for them, we are usually given another bag to put them in. Packaging protects the goods, but many items have extra, unnecessary packaging to make the product look bigger or more attractive, so that we choose it from the wide variety of goods that are available.

Once the product is unwrapped, the packaging becomes garbage. Some packaging materials, like glass and paper, can be recycled, but manufacturers also make packaging from mixtures of materials that cannot be easily recycled. Materials must be separated before they can be recycled; a cardboard carton cannot be recycled if it has plastic or metal stuck to it.

Wasting resources

Many of the things we buy have been made from the earth's raw materials. For instance, paper products and much of our furniture are made from wood. Wood is a renewable resource because new trees will grow to replace the ones we cut down. However, if logging companies cut down

trees faster than new ones can grow, wood becomes a scarce resource. Tropical hardwood timber is of high quality and is used in building and to make furniture, among other things. The rainforests of Southeast Asia have been the source of much of this valuable wood. But hardwood trees take hundreds of years to grow. Logging companies are felling trees at such a rate that some types of tree are nearly extinct. Unless trees are replanted or goods made from wood are reused, we could run out of this resource.

Other products are made from materials we dig out of the earth, like metals, oil, and coal. These are not renewable: they will not be replaced when we have used them up. Oil is the raw material from which many products are made, including plastics, pesticides, and the fibers used to make carpets. If we go on using oil at the present rate, the known reserves will only last for another thirty years. There are larger stores of other materials, like iron and aluminum, but they will all run out eventually.

Nonrenewable resources also supply energy for the manufacturing industries. Most of this energy comes from burning fossil fuels – coal, oil, and natural gas. We are using these up so fast that by the end of the next century we will be left with only a limited supply of coal.

The growing population

The world's population stands at five billion – more than double what it was in 1945. The number of people grows by about 230,000 every day. The population has been rapidly rising over the years as health care has improved and people have begun to live longer. However, in the developing countries of the world, many people are so poverty-stricken that their health suffers. These regions, in Africa, Asia, and Latin America, have the fastest rising populations because families have many children in case they do not all survive. Poor countries face basic, but serious, waste problems. As their populations rise, many places cannot even afford to collect and treat their sewage, much less their industrial waste.

However, the industrialized areas of Europe, North America, and Japan dwarf the poorer nations when it comes to producing waste and pollution, despite the fact that they hold only a quarter of the world's population. These areas consume 50 percent of the world's energy and 80 percent of all metals. Most of what is consumed ends up as waste – the amount of waste produced in these countries has reached 10 tons per person per year. It is proving difficult to dispose of all this waste, even though these countries are wealthy and can afford modern disposal techniques.

◁ As Mexico City's population increases, its pollution problems get worse.

Waste, resources, and pollution

The problem with waste is that it never actually disappears. Even if it is burned, buried, or dumped, in one form or another it remains to plague us. Waste is created at each stage of the manufacturing process, from mining to supplying electricity. Even the goods that are produced get thrown away when they are finished with. This is very wasteful of resources. Industry and individuals must be less wasteful and recycle more so that we can recover valuable resources and reduce the problems waste causes.

INDUSTRIES PROVIDE GOODS AND CREATE WASTE.

Power stations supply energy for homes and industries.

Raw materials

Metals, coal, and oil are essential for making goods and electricity, but extracting them causes problems. Mining leaves huge piles of rock, while oil wells can burn or leak oil into the sea.

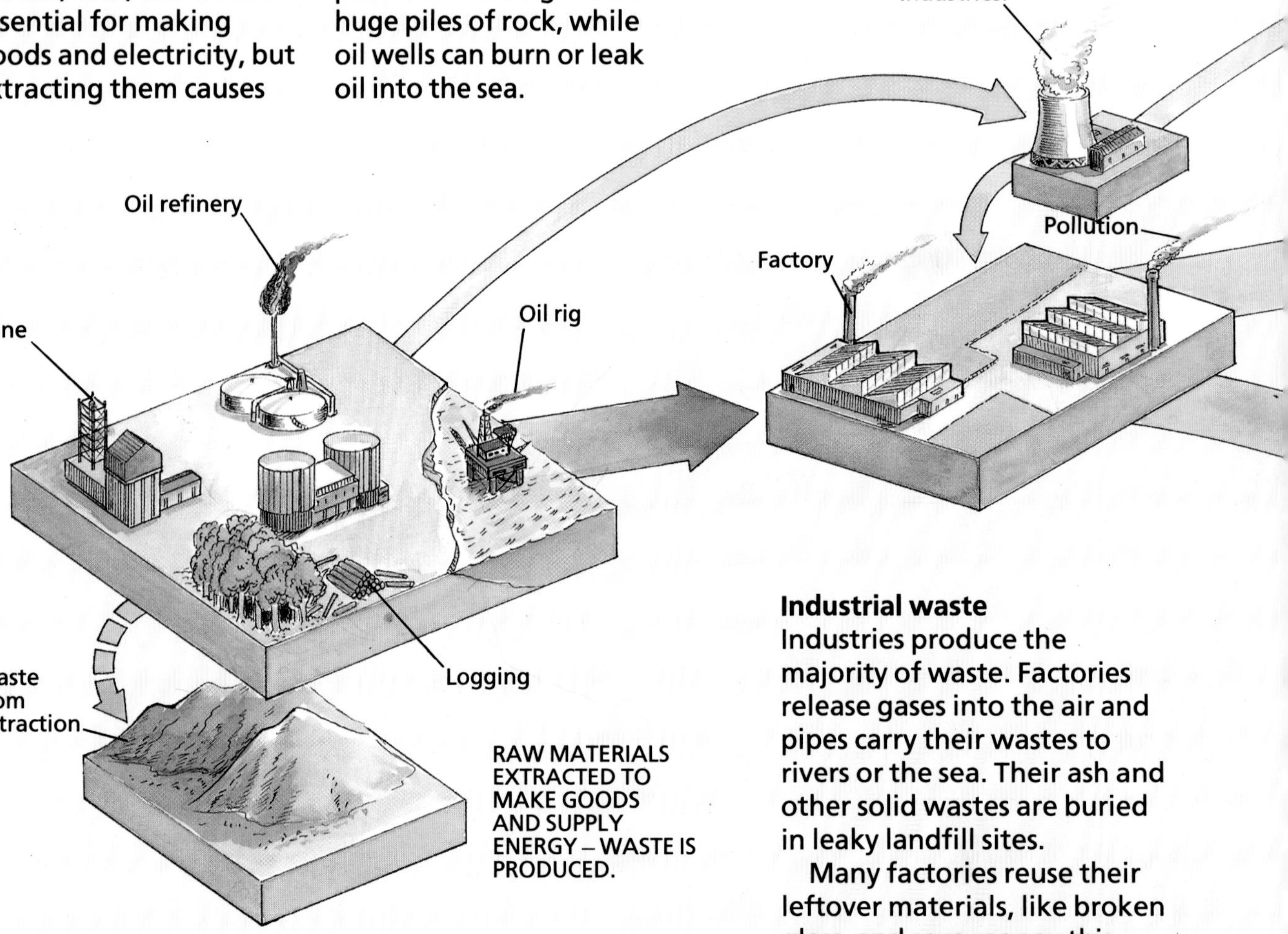

Oil refinery

Mine

Oil rig

Factory

Pollution

Waste from extraction

Logging

RAW MATERIALS EXTRACTED TO MAKE GOODS AND SUPPLY ENERGY – WASTE IS PRODUCED.

Industrial waste

Industries produce the majority of waste. Factories release gases into the air and pipes carry their wastes to rivers or the sea. Their ash and other solid wastes are buried in leaky landfill sites.

Many factories reuse their leftover materials, like broken glass, and save money this way. They can also reduce the amount of hazardous waste they produce by reusing cleaning materials like acids.

Fossil fuels

Fossil fuels provide almost all of our energy. Oil is also the raw material from which many useful chemicals, like drugs, and materials, like nylon, are made. But we extract fossil fuels at such a rate that they are rapidly running out.

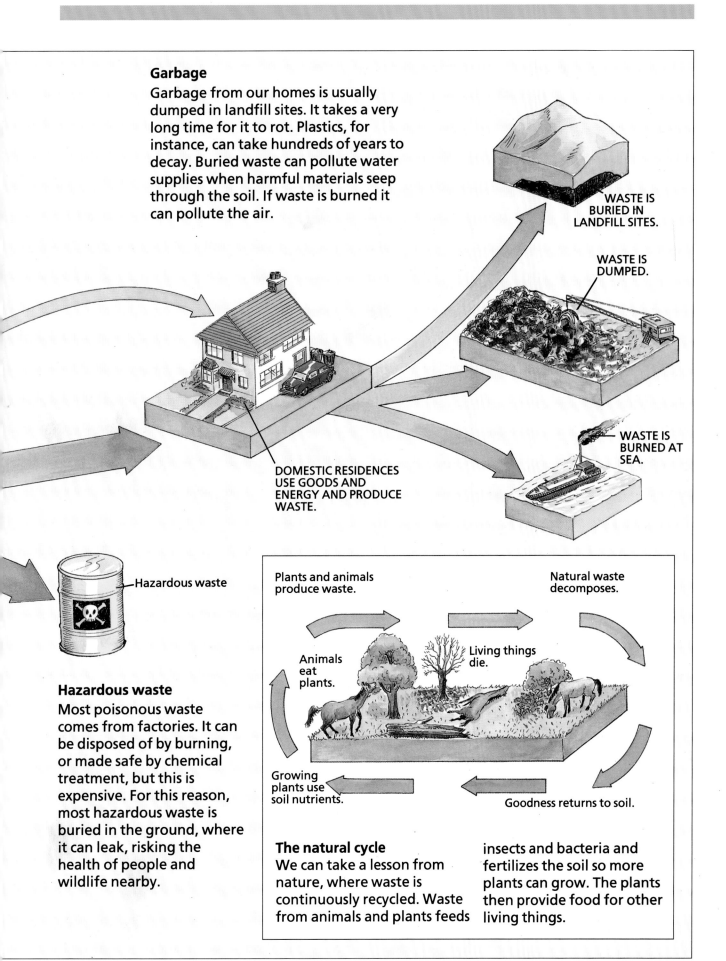

Garbage

Garbage from our homes is usually dumped in landfill sites. It takes a very long time for it to rot. Plastics, for instance, can take hundreds of years to decay. Buried waste can pollute water supplies when harmful materials seep through the soil. If waste is burned it can pollute the air.

WASTE IS BURIED IN LANDFILL SITES.

WASTE IS DUMPED.

WASTE IS BURNED AT SEA.

DOMESTIC RESIDENCES USE GOODS AND ENERGY AND PRODUCE WASTE.

Hazardous waste

Hazardous waste

Most poisonous waste comes from factories. It can be disposed of by burning, or made safe by chemical treatment, but this is expensive. For this reason, most hazardous waste is buried in the ground, where it can leak, risking the health of people and wildlife nearby.

Plants and animals produce waste.

Natural waste decomposes.

Animals eat plants.

Living things die.

Growing plants use soil nutrients.

Goodness returns to soil.

The natural cycle

We can take a lesson from nature, where waste is continuously recycled. Waste from animals and plants feeds insects and bacteria and fertilizes the soil so more plants can grow. The plants then provide food for other living things.

Chapter Two

THE PROBLEMS WITH WASTE

We are faced with accumulating amounts of waste that need to be disposed of. Most solid wastes are buried in the ground, where some things like old food and paper can decompose. But these sites fill up fast. Another problem with burying waste is that harmful chemicals from old bleach bottles and other discarded garbage can seep into water supplies. Waste from industries and sewage from homes are regularly disposed of by piping them into rivers or the sea, where they can kill wildlife and make people ill. Gases from cars, homes, industries, and power plants drift into the air where they are causing a whole series of problems. We may think we are disposing of our waste, but we are actually storing up trouble for the future.

Household garbage

Garbage from our homes is taken away regularly and we forget about it. Nearly half of our garbage is paper, but there are also glass jars, cans, plastic wrapping, garden clippings, leftover food, and many other items. The amount we throw out is staggering, and it costs billions of dollars to deal with it all. New York City alone throws out 24,000 tons of garbage every day.

About 80 percent of household garbage could be used again or made into something new. Glass, paper, cardboard, metals, including aluminum, and some plastics can be recycled with considerable savings of raw materials and energy. Recycling has been increasingly taken up as an alternative to dumping garbage. Bottle banks and collection points for paper and cans are now a common sight. But these measures have not been enough to counter the vast amount

◁ Landfill sites fill up rapidly, and suitable areas for new sites are difficult to find.

Industrial solid waste

Domestic garbage is only a tiny amount of the total solid waste. Industry produces much more. Britain produces 100 million tons of industrial waste every year. Most of this consists of paper, ash, metal, and plastic, and is no more dangerous than domestic waste. Only 10 to 20 percent of all industrial waste is considered hazardous. The biggest percentage of industrial waste is rock and slag from mines. These are dug out of the ground and are left after the coal or metal has been extracted. Piles of mining waste can cause pollution when the rain washes their contents into water supplies.

Landfill sites

The majority of solid waste is put in landfills. Garbage is packed into holes in the ground to take up as little space as possible and is then covered with soil. Once the site is filled and has settled, the area can be used to build a park or golf course. If the price of land is low, landfill sites are one of the cheapest disposal methods.

One drawback of landfill sites is that when it rains or snows, water can dissolve materials in the garbage, resulting in polluted water called leachate. This seeps down into the ground and can eventually pollute underground water, which is often the source of drinking water. Some sites are required by law to be lined with plastic or clay to prevent substances escaping into the ground, but ordinary domestic garbage dumps are not always lined. Leachate pollution can be prevented if the contaminated water is collected and drained away for treatment.

Another problem is that rotting garbage can produce explosive gases (mainly methane) which are dangerous if they seep into nearby buildings. The gases can also be

of wastes that need to be disposed of.

People often discard larger things like pieces of furniture, domestic appliances, and cars. Many old ovens, refrigerators, and washing machines are just dumped, even though scrap metal is valuable. There is a thriving industry that salvages metals from car bodies so that they can be used again.

Car tires cause greater problems because there are so many of them, and rubber is not as valuable as metal. In the United States, 240 million tires are thrown away every year. Some are recycled to make doormats, pipes, and rubberized pavement, but the majority just pile up on enormous dumps. One such dump in Canada containing 14 million tires caught fire and burned for two weeks. The burning rubber gave off thick, black smoke and poisonous gases, and left behind a hazardous oily liquid that had to be cleaned up.

△ The waste that overflows from New York City's dumps has to be carried away by barge.

a risk if they become trapped when the landfill site is covered, because they can cause explosions. The best modern sites pipe away the gases, which can then be burned to provide energy.

A few countries still allow liquid industrial wastes to be dumped in landfills containing domestic garbage. The solid garbage is supposed to soak up the liquid and stop it from draining into the soil. However, the mixture of materials can cause fires. In addition, poisonous gases can escape when different wastes react together.

We are running out of suitable places for landfill sites. The sites that already exist are filling up rapidly; some are already full. In New York the problem is acute. In 1987, a huge barge loaded with 3,100 tons of New York garbage sailed along the United States coastline for months trying to find a landfill site that would take its load. It was turned away from six sites before it was finally accepted – back in New York. Recently, New York has considered exporting its garbage to landfill sites in Britain because waste disposal is more expensive in the United States. However, even though

Britain is cheaper, it still costs 1.6 million dollars a day to dispose of British waste in landfill sites.

Incineration

As landfill sites become scarce and expensive, other ways to deal with our vast piles of waste have grown more popular. Burning garbage in an incinerator reduces the amount of solid waste by about 80 to 90 percent. Incineration is used to get rid of about 75 percent of Denmark's waste and about half the household garbage in Japan, Sweden, and Switzerland. The heat from the burning waste often provides heating or electricity for the nearby area.

Burning waste seems an ideal answer to the waste problem, but it does have drawbacks. Incineration is the most expensive form of waste disposal – over three times as costly as landfill sites. Furthermore, for every 10 tons of waste burned, one ton of ash remains. This may still contain harmful materials that pollute the environment when the ash is buried in landfill sites.

Incineration can also cause air pollution if

the gases from the burning garbage are released. Very high temperatures are needed to destroy plastics completely. If they are burned at lower temperatures, plastics that contain chlorine can give off poisonous gases called dioxins. These give people severe skin disease and are believed to cause cancer and birth defects as well. Sweden tightened its regulations on burning garbage when high levels of dioxins were found in some foods, thought to be partly caused by incinerators. With proper controls, the gases from incinerators can be cleaned to make this method of waste disposal quite safe.

Sewage
Most homes in industrialized countries are connected to sewers by an underground pipe which carries away dirty water from toilets, sinks and baths. The water and solids flow to a sewage plant where the sewage is cleaned and the liquid separated from the solids. The clean water is returned to a river or the sea. The solid sludge can be dried and sold as fertilizer.

In some places, particularly near coasts and large rivers, sewage is sometimes piped into the water without being treated. Approximately 90 percent of the sewage produced around the Mediterranean coastline is discharged untreated into the sea. Small amounts of sewage can decompose naturally, but the millions of tons of sewage we produce overwhelm nature's recycling systems. In addition, sewage contains harmful bacteria and small quantities of poisonous chemicals like bleaches and detergents, which people pour down their drains. Even if piped away from beaches, bacteria from human sewage contaminate many vacation resorts, resulting in illness among vacationers. There are many cities and towns along coasts around the world where sewage has made beaches too dirty for safe bathing.

In parts of the developing world, sewage is a much more serious problem. Poor areas cannot afford sewage treatment plants, so very little sewage is cleaned before it is discharged. The sewage systems that do exist are often overloaded because urban areas have grown enormously in recent years. In Bangkok, Thailand, less than 2 percent of homes are connected to the city's sewers. Thus, raw sewage often gets into rivers, which are also the source of drinking water. Some 94 percent of Ethiopians lack clean water. Serious diseases are caused in this way, including cholera and diarrhea. Nearly five million children die each year from diarrhea – about ten every minute. Dirty water is one of the world's greatest killers.

△ Raw sewage is washed onto British beaches from the sea, creating a health hazard.

Liquid waste from industry

Factories often pipe their liquid waste into sewers. This adds a variety of chemicals to sewage which the treatment plants cannot remove. Some of these chemicals can even kill the bacteria that are used to break down the sewage. Industrial liquids can contain many pollutants, for instance, poisonous heavy metals like mercury, which can cause nerve damage and birth defects. Sewage sludge with traces of heavy metals cannot be used as a fertilizer on farms because it would contaminate the crops. Even if it is used to feed forests, parks, or gardens, the heavy metals could damage the plants. Industrial waste can turn potentially useful fertilizer into a disposal problem. The only thing to do with contaminated sewage is burn or bury it.

Some industries on the banks of rivers discharge their liquid waste into them. Rivers all over the world have been damaged by this method of waste disposal. In China each year, 80 percent of the country's 37 billion tons of industrial and domestic waste is discharged into rivers and lakes without being treated. In 1988, waste built up in shellfish beds near Shanghai and gave 300,000 people who ate the shellfish hepatitis, an inflammation of the liver.

Wildlife also suffers from water pollution. Oil waste is one of the biggest threats to marine life. It clogs the feathers of birds so they cannot float or keep warm, and it poisons animals who swallow it. Most oil pollution is caused by ships illegally flushing out waste oil from their tanks, and by land-based industries dumping oil down drains. Accidents that cause oil spills are well publicized, but are not the major cause of oil pollution.

Farming waste

In the last 50 years, pollution from farming has caused growing concern. Agriculture has had to supply more and more food for

△ For this family in Nepal, a weed-choked pool supplies water for washing.

the growing population. Modern methods of farming are more efficient at producing food, but they also create more waste problems. For example, many modern farms keep hundreds of livestock inside large buildings where they can be cared for easily. These animals produce large quantities of manure. In the past, the manure from grazing animals would go to fertilize the crops. But if the huge amounts of manure produced now are spread on the land, it cannot decompose. The excess gets washed off by the rain into rivers or underground water supplies.

Farmers store the manure in slurry pits before it is put on the fields. The slurry sometimes leaks into rivers and streams and contaminates them. The Netherlands has so much manure from the country's 14 million hogs that farmers had to reduce their herds.

△ An oil tanker blazes, turning a resource into a waste.

Slurry and sewage are damaging when they seep into rivers and the oceans because they supply food for water plants like algae, causing them to grow and multiply quickly. When the algae die and decompose they use up oxygen from the water, suffocating fish and other living things. This process is called eutrophication. In the last few years, algal blooms caused by too much sewage in the North Sea and in the Mediterranean have resulted in massive fish kills.

Pesticides and fertilizers
Modern farming relies on the use of chemicals like pesticides and fertilizers. Pesticides poison insect pests, kill weeds, and stop the spread of diseases that damage crops. These chemicals have increased food production around the world, but we are beginning to realize that they cause environmental damage.

To be effective, large amounts of pesticides are sprayed onto crops. Rain and wind carry the excess pesticides into the soil and into waterways. This pollution can be dangerous to wildlife. Some pesticides are stored in body fat and become more concentrated as larger creatures eat smaller ones. In this way animals of prey can build up harmful levels of pesticides, some of which can cause cancer. In many places, drinking water already contains minute amounts of pesticides. At present, little is known about the effects of pesticides on human health, but they are designed to be poisons. Some scientists believe they can cause cancer if they are consumed.

Chemical fertilizers are artificial plant food. They would not cause any problems if plants absorbed it all, but excess fertilizer can be washed into rivers and groundwater. Fertilizers contain nitrates, which are

△ Spraying pesticides by air is wasteful and dangerous, as some of the chemicals blow away.

thought to cause a range of health problems. Several European countries have high levels of nitrates in their drinking water as a result of fertilizer pollution. In addition, nitrates cause eutrophication in water habitats in the same way as sewage and slurry do. The Pantanal wetland in Brazil is being slowly poisoned as large quantities of fertilizers from farms seep into the marshes, threatening some of the region's rare wildlife.

Polluting the air
The atmosphere is a very valuable resource. Without clean air to breathe, we could not survive. But even the atmosphere has not been able to escape the wastes humans produce. Smoke and gases from factories and power plants, and exhaust fumes from vehicles are causing widespread damage to the environment, and are affecting our own health. Worldwide, air pollution causes at least 150,000 deaths a year.

Each exhaust pipe on the world's 400 million cars sends waste gases into the air.

Residents of cities in sunny regions suffer from smog caused by gases from car exhausts. In places like Los Angeles, Athens, Mexico City, and Sydney, sunshine makes the gases react together to produce ozone. Although a layer of ozone in the

Long-lived waste
DDT is a pesticide which was hailed as a miracle when it was first introduced. It has been used all over the world, especially to kill mosquitoes that spread malaria. But it is poisonous and lingers in the environment long after use. It builds up in the bodies of birds and animals, and causes breeding problems. This nearly led to the extinction of some birds of prey, like the osprey. DDT has now been banned in many countries, but will continue to affect the environment in the future.

atmosphere protects us from the sun's dangerous radiation, at ground level, ozone is a poisonous gas that damages plantlife. It also gives people eye and lung problems. On some days in Mexico City, breathing the air causes the same damage to the lungs as smoking two packs of cigarettes a day.

Factories and power plants that burn fossil fuels, like coal and oil, are also responsible for polluting the air. Waste gases from their chimneys contain chemicals that cause coughing and other lung problems. In the last decades, the industrialized countries have made progress in cleaning up the air by passing laws to regulate pollution. But governments have not taken action quickly enough to prevent long-term environmental problems.

Acid rain

Waste gases in the atmosphere form acid rain, which is causing widespread damage to buildings, forests, lakes and rivers. Most acid rain is caused by sulfur dioxide and nitrogen oxides, which result from burning fossil fuels in factories, cars, and power plants. Much of these wastes drop to the ground where they are produced, but some drift up and react with water vapor in the clouds to make sulfuric and nitric acids. These can be carried thousands of miles by the wind to fall as acid rain in other countries. The United States exports acid rain to Canada, and Britain's acid rain falls on Scandinavia.

Acid rain washes the nutrients out of the soil and damages trees and plantlife. It also makes lakes and rivers too acidic for fish to survive. In Sweden, fish in 4,000 lakes have been killed by acid rain, and in Norway over half the trout population has been lost. More than half of German and Dutch forests have been damaged by acid rain.

Although the problem of acid rain is not new (the name was first used in 1872 in Manchester), it has escalated since 1945.

△ Food crops will fail if global warming significantly alters the climate.

The amounts of sulfur dioxide and nitrogen oxides released into the air from Europe doubled between 1950 and 1970. These waste gases can be reduced. Car exhaust gases can be cleaned by devices called catalytic converters, and sulfur dioxide can be trapped in factory chimneys.

Global warming

The earth is able to sustain life as we know it because of the Greenhouse Effect. This is the process by which carbon dioxide and other gases in the atmosphere trap the sun's heat and keep the planet warm. Every year we produce billions of tons of these gases when we burn fossil fuels. The quantity of carbon dioxide in the atmosphere has gradually increased since the beginning of industrialization a couple of hundred years ago. Scientists fear that this will make the whole world warmer.

This change in climate, called global warming, would cause sea levels to rise as water expands and ice caps melt, flooding low-lying areas. Also, some areas would become hotter and drier and others much wetter. It may be difficult for humans, plants and wildlife to adapt to the changing conditions. So the wastes we produce every day could ultimately disrupt the environment of the entire planet.

Chapter Three

DANGEROUS WASTE

Some of the waste we produce is deadly. Waste that is explosive, liable to burst into flames, give off gases, or cause chemical burns is called hazardous waste. This includes toxic waste, which is poisonous. Radioactive waste, produced mainly by the nuclear power and nuclear weapons industries, is also dangerous. Although the proportion of hazardous waste is small compared with the total amount of waste we produce, it is so dangerous that it has caused many problems. Various methods of dealing with this waste have been developed, and some dangerous waste can even be recycled. But the dumps where these wastes were buried before their dangers were fully realized remain extremely dangerous.

Hazardous waste

About 90 percent of hazardous waste is produced by industries. Many of the products that we rely on – plastics, soap, fertilizers, medicines, detergents, cosmetics, paints, and pesticides – create toxic waste when they are manufactured. Medical waste from hospitals can also be hazardous because it may contain powerful drugs or could spread diseases.

Some of the products we throw away at home are also hazardous. Paint thinner, cleaning materials, and disposable cigarette lighters that contain unused fuel are all considered hazardous waste. Even old television sets on a waste dump can leak poisonous chemicals.

Different countries have their own definition of what toxic waste is, so it is impossible to know how much is produced. For instance, the Netherlands and Belgium do not agree at what level cyanide, a powerful poison, becomes dangerous. Furthermore, some countries do not even

◁ When toxic waste is burned at sea, the smoke and gases are allowed to escape, polluting the air and the water. The ash is also dumped in the ocean, causing more pollution. This caused an outcry among environmentalists, leading to incineration being banned in the North Sea.

keep records of what waste they produce, and many chemicals have not yet been tested to see if they affect human health.

The vast majority of all hazardous waste is produced in the industrialized countries. The United States produces approximately 260 million tons each year (not including radioactive waste) – more than one ton per person. It is essential that all this waste is disposed of where it cannot harm people or the environment. Some is buried in special landfill sites that are lined either with thick layers of clay or with tough plastic, to prevent the hazardous materials from escaping into the environment. Many dangerous wastes can be treated chemically to make them less harmful, and then dumped in landfill sites.

The problem is that it is practically impossible to keep the hazardous materials within landfill sites. Certain chemicals can dissolve any lining material, allowing the waste to leak into the soil. Heavy rainstorms can flood the site, and the overflowing water can carry hazardous materials into the environment. These problems have led the United States to phase out landfilling of hazardous waste, while some other countries only allow it for materials that are less dangerous.

Burning toxic wastes
The amount of hazardous waste can be vastly reduced by incineration. Modern toxic waste incinerators burn at very high temperatures and, when operated correctly, can destroy at least 99.99 percent of the dangerous materials. To do this the incinerator must be kept at the correct temperature for the right length of time, and the waste needs to be thoroughly mixed to ensure that it all burns completely. However, some substances, like heavy metals, cannot be destroyed by burning. Other dangerous materials, like dioxins, can be created during incineration. These can either escape from the chimney or can remain in the ash, which is buried.

For this reason, people near incinerators fear that their health might be affected, although it is difficult to prove that specific health problems have been caused by incinerators. Another worry is that human negligence or equipment failure could cause the release of toxic gases.

The risks to people can be reduced if hazardous waste is burned at sea. In the 1980s, about 100,000 tons a year were burned at sea by Belgium, Britain, France, and Germany. Ocean incineration is much cheaper than land incineration, because the gases that are released do not have to be cleaned. Environmentalists claimed that these toxic gases could be carried by the wind to land or could affect marine life. They also argued that accidents or shipwrecks could spill the dangerous materials. These arguments were heeded, and incineration in the North Sea was banned in 1991.

Persistent waste

Dumping hazardous wastes directly into the sea is also now banned, except for tiny quantities in sewage sludge or sediment dredged from river and seabeds. However, even small amounts can be dangerous, because some of these materials persist in the environment for a long time. One example is PCBs (polychlorinated biphenyls). These have been used since the 1930s, particularly in heavy electrical equipment. Their danger was first realized in 1968, when 1,300 people in Japan suffered from severe skin problems and liver and kidney damage as a result of eating rice oil contaminated by PCBs. Production of PCBs was stopped in many countries, but they can still leak from old equipment.

About 30 percent of all the PCBs ever produced have already leaked into the environment (20 percent into the oceans and 10 percent into soils), and they have now spread to remote areas far from any

Disposing of chemical weapons
The Gulf War in 1991 brought the world's attention to chemical weapons. These are bombs which contain deadly chemicals that can burn human skin or can be fatal if inhaled. Large stockpiles of these exist which are too old to be used, but could still be very dangerous. The United States has built an incinerator on Johnston Island in the Pacific Ocean to get rid of some of these weapons. Many people in the area are worried that poisonous gases could escape when these chemicals are burned.

△ An American soldier prepares chemical weapons for incineration on Johnston Island in the Pacific Ocean.

△ The substances in industrial waste dumps can be so harmful that the workers have to protect themselves with special clothing and equipment.

industrial site. Traces of PCBs have even been found in Arctic snow. PCBs can only be destroyed by incineration.

Dangerous dumps

The chemical industry produces the largest proportion of toxic waste. As this industry has expanded, so has the amount of dangerous waste. Before the 1970s, most of the wastes were just dumped, with no attempt to prevent them leaking out into the environment. There were few regulations because no one realized how much damage they could do.

Some countries have now carried out surveys of these old sites. The United States holds many abandoned toxic waste sites, 10,000 of which need immediate cleanup to stop them from endangering human lives.

In Germany, 6,000 dumps have been closed because they are dangerous, and the cost of cleaning these up will be thousands of millions of Deutschmarks. The United States has set up a "superfund" to pay for cleaning up dangerous dumps, but it does not cover the cost of cleaning up even the sites that are known now, let alone others that may be found in the future.

Unfortunately, one of the ways leaking waste dumps are discovered is when they begin to make people ill. There are many kinds of hazardous wastes and each type affects health in a different way. PCBs and the heavy metal cadmium, found in batteries and some fertilizers, cause cancers in animals and humans. Mercury, which has many industrial uses, can cause birth defects and can affect the nervous system.

Direct contact with some materials causes burns, and fumes can damage the lungs or the eyes. Different materials attack different parts of the body, from the skin to the brain. The liver, kidneys, and heart are especially vulnerable. Some materials are so toxic that they are fatal even in small doses.

Waste disasters

The incident that jarred the world into recognizing the dangers of toxic waste is known as the disaster of Love Canal. From 1930 to 1950, a chemical company used an uncompleted canal near Niagara Falls in New York State as a waste dump for over 22,000 tons of chemicals. In 1953 the dump was filled in with earth and then sold, and a school and houses were built on it.

In 1976, heavy rain and snow caused the chemicals to leak into gardens and basements of houses, burning children who came into contact with them. Worried residents found that an abnormally high proportion of pregnant women were having miscarriages. Of those babies that were born, more than the average number had birth defects. Love Canal was declared a disaster area in 1978, and around 250 families were evacuated. There are more than 200 other toxic waste dumps near Niagara Falls. One, containing a ton of highly poisonous dioxin, is close to the Niagara River, which supplies drinking water to six million people.

Another tragedy occurred on the west coast of Japan in the 1960s. Waste that contained cadmium was released from zinc-refining industries and mines into the Zintsu River. Water from the river was used for drinking water and to irrigate crops. The cadmium in drinking water and people's food weakened their bones, which would break at the slightest movement. Several hundred people died from this condition, called *itai-itai* disease (Japanese for "it hurts, it hurts").

In these two extreme cases, people lost their homes or died because of carelessly dumped toxic waste. More often, the harmful effects of hazardous waste are suspected, but cannot be proved. There is some evidence that landfill sites may have effects that are less noticeable, but more widespread. Some areas of the United States that have high concentrations of chemical dumps also have higher rates of cancer. In highly industrialized areas of Poland, pollution is unregulated. The life expectancy in these areas is lower than

△ In 1986, toxic chemicals spilled into the Rhine River, killing water life, like eels.

elsewhere in Poland, and children suffer more often from diseases like leukemia (a kind of cancer).

Nuclear waste

Radioactive waste is created when electricity is generated in nuclear power plants. For many people, nuclear waste is the most frightening of hazardous wastes, even though only a small amount is highly dangerous and this is disposed of very carefully. Nuclear waste is dangerous because it produces radiation, which can harm living cells.

Radioactive waste is usually divided into three classes, depending on the amount and danger of the radiation emitted. The bulk of nuclear waste is classed as low-level and is not very harmful. It includes clothing, paper towels, and other equipment that has been in contact with radiation. Intermediate-level waste is more radioactive and includes the material that surrounds the fuel in nuclear power plants. High-level waste is extremely radioactive – and dangerous. It consists mainly of the used fuel from nuclear power plants.

Nuclear waste cannot be destroyed. It gradually loses its radioactivity over time, but intermediate- and high-level waste will remain dangerous for thousands of years. For this period it must be shielded to prevent radiation from escaping. Low- and intermediate-level wastes are often enclosed in steel and concrete and stored underground, but there is no generally accepted way of safely storing high-level waste. Usually it is encased in steel and concrete and put in tanks of water to keep it cool. It can also be converted into glass blocks, which will take up less space and be easier to handle. A plant for this purpose opened in 1991 at Sellafield in Britain. These glass blocks will still need very secure storage. Because high-level waste must be stored for many thousands of years before it is safe, the amount to be stored will continue to accumulate.

△ Containers of high-level radioactive waste are kept cool in storage tanks.

Even if every precaution is taken to store nuclear waste safely, the risk of accidents or leaks can never be ruled out. So far, the only known disaster at a nuclear waste storage site was at Kyshtym in the Soviet Union in 1957, where an explosion contaminated 15,000 sq km (5,800 sq mi) with radiation. Some 10,000 people were evacuated from the area, and hundreds of people are believed to have died.

Recycling nuclear fuel

The fuel used to generate electricity in nuclear power plants is uranium. It becomes less efficient after a few years of use and has to be replaced. The used fuel rods are extremely radioactive, but they still contain a lot of useful uranium which can be processed into new fuel. They are sent to a special plant where the uranium and plutonium are extracted, and this process is called reprocessing.

Reprocessing recycles the uranium and reduces the original amount of high-level waste. Only about three percent of the original used fuel is left as a highly radioactive liquid waste. However, reprocessing produces 10 times the volume of intermediate-level waste and 100 times the volume of low-level waste. Another drawback is the risk involved in transporting the used fuel from the power plants to the reprocessing plants. It is transported by road, rail, and ship across Europe, and even from Japan to plants in Britain and France. Although heavy steel containers are used that have been tested to ensure they will not break, accidents are not entirely impossible.

There have also been several radiation leaks from the reprocessing plants themselves, and Sellafield in Britain drains low-level radioactive waste into the Irish Sea. These factors, together with the cost of reprocessing, mean that many countries choose to store their used fuel at the power plant instead of reprocessing it. Either way, radioactive waste remains an enormous disposal problem.

Exporting poisonous waste

To save money, some industries deal with their waste by exporting it to countries that do not insist on costly disposal procedures. Poor countries in the developing world accept waste as a way of earning money, but they seldom have the facilities to dispose of it safely. Europe and the United States export waste to African countries and some Asian countries,

△ Highly radioactive used nuclear fuel is transported by rail and ship to be reprocessed.

including China. This trade occurs legally, but some irresponsible companies also dump waste illegally. In Nigeria in 1988, 3,500 tons of dangerous materials from Italy were illegally dumped on a farmer's property. Almost half the containers were leaking, resulting in a high risk of fire or explosion. They were also contaminating the local supply of drinking water.

Ships containing dangerous waste are often turned away from ports as unacceptable risks. Several have hit the headlines in past years, including the *Karin B.*, which toured around European ports for months in 1988 before it was forced to take its lethal cargo back to Italy, where it originally came from. Other ships have had to stay at sea for even longer. One carried contaminated sludge from the United States for two years. Another cargo of waste traveled around for a year until the leaking drums made eight crewmen ill.

The regulations in Europe covering the export of hazardous waste are being tightened to ensure that the receiving country is properly informed and can handle the waste safely. This will create problems in Europe, which at present can only deal safely with about a third of its hazardous wastes. Japan has shown one way forward, by recycling half of the toxic waste it produces, but the best alternative would be to use manufacturing methods that create less waste in the first place.

△ Barrels of toxic waste can leak while in storage, contaminating the area.

Recycling and waste

At present only a fraction of all waste is recycled. Most of this recycling is done within industry. But at least half of the materials in our household garbage could be salvaged and used again. The useful materials that are thrown away every year are worth hundreds of millions of dollars. Apart from this waste of money and natural resources, using recycled materials often reduces pollution. Recycling can cost the individual a little extra time and money, but in the long run we will benefit from doing it.

United States

35% of steel recycled

Europe

42% of aluminum recycled

China

9% of steel recycled

Paper

About half of domestic garbage is paper, which can be recycled into toilet rolls and egg boxes. Better-quality waste paper from offices can be made into printing and writing paper. In Europe, almost a third of new paper products are made from recycled materials. Each ton of paper recycled saves about 15 average-sized trees.

Food and drink cans

Most cans are not made of pure aluminum. They are made of a mixture of metals, often steel with a thin coating of tin. These metals can be separated and recycled many times, which saves energy and reduces pollution. Making aluminum from raw materials uses 20 times the energy needed for recycling, and produces 20 times as much air and water pollution.

Paper recycled

Philippines — 16%

Mexico — 45%

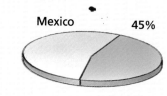

Plastics

Plastics used in industry can be profitably recycled, but plastics in household garbage are more of a problem. Many plastic items are made of a mixture of materials that are difficult to separate. But plastic bags and containers can often be reused many times.

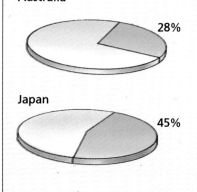

Australia — 28%

Japan — 45%

100 cans of garbage are produced by each household in Europe every year.

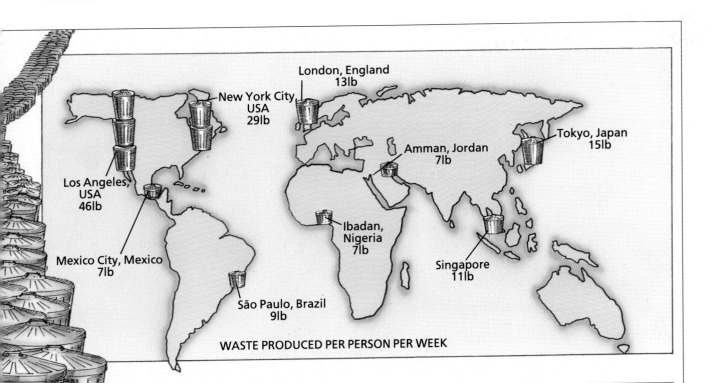

WASTE PRODUCED PER PERSON PER WEEK

London, England
13lb

New York City,
USA
29lb

Tokyo, Japan
15lb

Amman, Jordan
7lb

Los Angeles,
USA
46lb

Mexico City, Mexico
7lb

Ibadan,
Nigeria
7lb

Singapore
11lb

São Paulo, Brazil
9lb

Household garbage

The wealthy, industrialized countries produce far more waste than developing nations, partly because individuals throw away more. Many items in our garbage, like clothing and other textiles, can be reused. If they are not good enough to be sold in flea markets, they can be recycled to make mattress fillings, cleaning cloths, blankets, and carpets.

Glass

Glass can be recycled almost indefinitely. Although the raw materials to make glass are plentiful and cheap, the glass industry likes to buy glass from bottle banks because using recycled glass saves energy. It is even better to reuse glass containers, which is now encouraged in some countries.

Saving energy by recycling

Using recycled materials in manufacturing almost always saves money, particularly in the metals industry. This is because it takes large amounts of energy to extract metals.

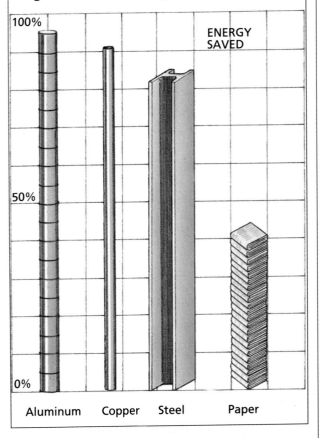

ENERGY SAVED

100%

50%

0%

Aluminum   Copper   Steel   Paper

Chapter Four

REDUCING AND RECYCLING WASTE

Industry and scientists are constantly developing new methods to deal with waste. BMW, the German car firm, has designed a car that is made entirely of recyclable materials. Around the world, an increasing number of communities and companies have been starting up recycling programs. However, waste is growing as a problem far more quickly than solutions are being implemented. The simplest and most effective way to reduce the problem of waste is to produce less of it, particularly the types that cannot be recycled. But beyond this, recycling must become standard practice. Governments must respond to the growing concern about waste and pass laws to ensure that as much waste as possible is recycled.

Reducing industrial waste

Often it takes only small changes in a manufacturing process to cut down on the industrial waste generated. Waste problems can sometimes be prevented by changing from toxic materials to nonpoisonous ones that will do the job equally well. A company that makes gift-wrapping paper eliminated its hazardous waste just by changing to a different type of ink – and saved itself $35,000 a year.

The 3M Company (Minnesota Mining and Manufacturing) in the United States was one of the first to reduce its overall waste. Since starting its pollution prevention program in 1975, it has halved its waste production and saved nearly $500 million. Many other companies have also

◁ Scrap metal is pressed into blocks for easier handling and storage. It will be melted down and made into new products.

▽ Waste polythene, a kind of plastic, is collected from industries and recycled into pellets to be used in the building industry.

found that reducing waste saves money. Still, a survey of large chemical companies in the United States showed that less than half had programs for waste reduction.

Scientists have also developed methods of reducing the problems of industrial waste. Hazardous oil waste can be converted into harmless substances by bacteria that occur naturally in the soil. Toxic waste containing chlorine can be made safe by bacteria that remove chlorine. These methods can also be used for nonhazardous waste. Millions of East German Trabant cars lie on dumps in Germany. Trabants are made from a wood pulp mixture which scientists believe can be broken down by bacteria and funghi. If this process works, it could be used on other waste as well.

Reusing industrial materials

Some industries, in particular the metal industry, have a long tradition of reusing and recycling materials within their factories to save money. For example, the trimmings left from the manufacture of copper pipes are collected and melted down to be used again. Acid used to clean steel during its manufacture becomes contaminated with iron, which is then separated out, leaving both the iron and acid for future use. The silver in photographic paper is also recovered and used again to coat new paper.

Many industries use toxic solvents, which dissolve other substances. In the United States there is a rapidly growing business worth $200 million a year that recycles industrial solvents. Some materials, while of no use to the factory that produces them, are valuable to other industries. Blast furnaces in the metal industry produce a waste material called slag, which is used in construction and road building. Waste exchanges are currently operating in Europe and the United States, where waste materials produced by one company are used as raw material for another industry. The 3M Company sells one of its toxic wastes to an industry that can use it to manufacture fertilizers. Both companies save money with this exchange. Britain and the Netherlands have been participating in waste exchange programs since the 1970s, with more than 150 substances listed for exchange.

Other waste products need processing before they become useful. Many power plant and factory chimneys release sulfur dioxide gas, which pollutes the atmosphere and contributes to acid rain. However, the gas can be trapped by mixing it with limestone, and then processed to convert it to gypsum. This can then be sold to the building industry. Other treatments can turn sulfur dioxide into sulfur or sulfuric acid, both needed by chemical industries. These processes can be costly to introduce, but the products can be sold to benefit the industry.

Reusing household garbage

The best way to reduce the garbage from our homes is to reuse things rather than throw them out. It is often possible to sell items that we no longer want at flea markets, or donate them to thrift shops, giving other people the chance to use them. If milk is delivered to the door in glass bottles instead of throw-away cartons, the bottles can be used twenty times on average. Some wine bottles in France are also reused. A small cash deposit is reclaimed when the bottles are returned.

△ Poor countries reuse old containers.

Deposit programs like this were much more popular in the past, but faded out as cheap plastic bottles and aluminum cans took over from glass bottles. They are beginning to make a comeback now as we become more aware of the damage pollution does to the environment. In Oregon in the United States, all drink containers carry a deposit to encourage their return for reuse or recycling. Denmark goes even further, banning aluminum cans. All drinks there must be sold in standard bottles with a returnable deposit, and all stores that sell drinks must also pay out deposits on returned bottles.

Recycling

Although items like empty jars and containers can be used many times, not

30

△ Many countries, like Portugal, collect paper and cardboard for recycling.

much of our garbage can be used again in its original form. Yet it does contain useful materials that could be made into new products. One of the major problems with recycling is separating these materials from the other garbage. There are recycling plants where mixed garbage can be sorted, partly by machine and partly by hand. However, it is much better if it is not mixed in the first place, which means we have to sort our garbage in our own homes. There are already programs in hundreds of cities where this is being tried, and the different materials are collected separately.

The valuable materials in household garbage are mainly glass, papers and metals. Many countries now have bottle banks where people can take their empty glass bottles, sorted by color, for recycling. Collection points for newspapers, cardboard, and aluminum cans are also being set up, and small, but growing numbers of people are using them. Manufacturers will collect and pay for these materials if enough are assembled in one place. In the United States, where vast numbers of aluminum drinks cans are made, over half are recycled, and in Switzerland 40 percent of used glass is recovered.

Recycling is expanding; in the United States the amount of paper recycled doubled each year from 1975 to 1980. Japan, Mexico, Spain, and the Netherlands recycle between 40 and 50 percent of their paper. Recycling not only saves valuable resources like wood and metals, but uses less energy than manufacturing products from raw materials, thus conserving the world's limited supply of fossil fuels. Although it is expensive to set up systems for collecting, sorting and transporting, recycling materials like aluminum, glass, and paper is still economic, especially as the prices of dwindling resources rise.

Quite a large proportion of domestic garbage is food scraps and vegetable peelings. This will decompose to make compost, which is a valuable fertilizer for the garden. In some German towns and cities, this garbage is collected and used in parks or taken to farms in the countryside. In one city in China, where eight million people produce 5,000 tons of garbage each day, hogs are used to consume the mountains of waste, and their manure goes to fertilize gardens and farms.

A few industries have well-established recycling programs, like the car-scrap business, which saves and reuses a wide range of parts and materials from cars. Yet recycling is still in its infancy. Only a minority of people recycle, and only a few local governments sort the valuable materials from mixed garbage. It is vital to expand these projects as resources become more scarce and waste clutters and damages the environment. However, there will always be some garbage that cannot be recycled because it is made from a mixture of materials: the only thing to do with this is to reduce it to a minimum.

Problems with plastics

It is not easy to recycle plastics because there are many different kinds. Some plastics melt when heated and can be remolded into new products. Others remain solid even at high temperatures. There are processes for making mixtures of these plastics into a limited number of products, like fence posts, but these cannot then be recycled again.

Some plastics can be recycled if they are separated from the other types. Research is being carried out to find ways of sorting plastics automatically. So far, it is quicker and more accurate to sort plastics by hand, the sorters learning to recognize the main types by sight. Sheffield in Britain has recently set up a major program to recycle garbage, but only about half the plastics are recycled. Some are contaminated with other substances and some types of plastics cannot be recycled yet.

In the United States there is a plant to recycle the polystyrene used as containers for hot drinks and food like hamburgers. After being checked for impurities and washed, the polystyrene is turned into pellets which are used to make new

△ A biogas tank in India produces methane.

32

Biogas
When domestic and farm wastes are allowed to rot in an airtight container they can provide a potentially useful gas. Rotting waste gives off a mixture of carbon dioxide and methane that can be burned to provide electricity or heating, or to run cars. The remaining waste is a useful fertilizer. Belgium and Italy already have successful biogas plants supplying energy. In China and other developing countries, biogas plants use animal dung, human sewage, and plant waste to provide energy for cooking and heating.

△ A Belgian scientist has discovered how to produce oil from highly compressed and heated kitchen garbage.

products like flowerpots. McDonald's, the hamburger chain, is collecting its used burger boxes and sending them to this plant for recycling. At the moment these projects are rare. It costs a lot to recycle plastic, and many people think it is better to burn it with other garbage that cannot be recycled, to provide energy.

New ways of thinking
We can no longer ignore waste. Garbage dumps are rapidly filling up and waste disposal is getting increasingly expensive.

Many old dumps lie near water supplies or towns and pose a danger to nearby residents. In the United States, between 1980 and 1985, there were 7,000 known accidents during the transportation of toxic waste by truck and rail, resulting in the deaths of 139 people. Disasters like this will increase unless a concerted effort is made to tackle the problem.

There are things we can do. Ordinary people can persuade industry to produce less waste by buying products that can be reused or recycled. We can also avoid buying things with too much unnecessary packaging. This will help because the manufacture and disposal of packaging creates waste. Paper bags and carriers generally last as long as they are needed, and can then be recycled. Some environmentally-aware stores have changed back to paper bags, while others encourage shoppers to bring back their plastic bags and use them many times. These are simple steps you can take yourself, and you can encourage your school, workplace, and family to take them as well.

Governments can do even more to encourage industries to reduce and recycle their waste, especially if the industries save money by doing so. A small tax on waste production would pay for the cost of researching and developing processes to reduce or recycle waste. In some European countries like France, the Netherlands, Denmark, and Germany, governments help to pay for research into programs that reduce pollution. France can also reuse its sewage sludge as fertilizer because it does not allow industrial effluent to be mixed with household sewage. Industrial liquid waste can only be discharged into the sewers if it has been treated to make it safe.

With strict new laws to prevent pollution, waste disposal is becoming much more expensive. Industry is beginning to see waste reduction and recycling as a cheaper

△ In Italy, woollen rags from all over the world are cleaned and recycled into new fabrics.

option. Industrialized countries can afford to install the latest environmentally-friendly technology, and they should take steps to do so. Also, everyone will benefit if these countries give assistance to the poorer nations to help them dispose of their waste safely and install clean industry.

As the public has become increasingly conscious of environmental issues, international agreements have been seen as one of the best ways to protect the planet. Many dangerous practices of the past have already been outlawed, like dumping of nuclear waste and hazardous waste at sea, and others are being phased out. Many nations have also agreed to limit the release of harmful gases to the atmosphere: CFCs that damage the ozone layer, sulfur dioxide that causes acid rain, and carbon dioxide that contributes to global warming. However, there is still much to be done to rectify the damage our wastes have caused. The hope for the future depends on people recognizing that controlling waste, and cleaning up what we have already produced, needs to be an urgent priority.

GLOSSARY

algal bloom rapid growth of tiny water plants that occurs when sewage or fertilizers get into the water and supply too much plant food.

CFCs (chlorofluorocarbons) gases that are used in refrigerators and the electronics industry. When they get into the atmosphere they damage the ozone layer.

consumer boom when people buy more goods, especially items they do not need. It is made possible by increasing wealth, and encouraged by advertising.

developing countries poorer countries with little industry, and economies based mainly around agriculture.

dioxins extremely poisonous chemicals that contain chlorine. They are created during the manufacture of paper and chemicals, and are also produced when plastics are burned at low temperatures.

eutrophication the removal of oxygen from water when large quantities of water plants like algae die and decay. This kills off other life, because without oxygen hardly anything can survive in the water.

global warming the gradual increase of the earth's temperature, due to the slow buildup in the atmosphere of the gases that keep the planet warm. This increase in gases is caused by human activities like burning fossil fuels.

Greenhouse Effect the natural process by which gases like carbon dioxide trap the sun's heat in the earth's atmosphere, keeping the planet warm enough for life.

hazardous waste waste that is poisonous if it is swallowed or inhaled, is explosive, liable to catch fire, or is dangerous in any other way. Most of this type of waste is produced by the chemicals and petroleum industries. Poisonous waste is also called toxic waste.

heavy metals include the metals mercury, lead, and cadmium. Some are poisonous and build up in the environment and in the bodies of people and animals.

incineration the burning of waste, often using the heat to generate electricity. Toxic waste incinerators must operate at very high temperatures, and the smoke must be cleaned to remove poisonous gases.

industrialized countries rich countries where industry provides more jobs than agriculture.

landfill an area of land where garbage is dumped, packed down, and covered with soil. Most domestic garbage and industrial waste is dumped in landfill sites.

leachate the liquid formed in landfill sites when water filters through the garbage, dissolving materials. This polluted water can contaminate rivers and groundwater.

nuclear radiation energetic particles that are given out when the nucleus of an atom breaks up. Materials that give out radiation are called radioactive. Radiation can harm living things by damaging cells.

PCBs (polychlorinated biphenyls) toxic materials used in heavy electrical goods. They are long-lived and cause problems when they get into the environment.

pollution any substance that harms the environment.

recycling reclaiming the useful materials from waste so that they can be used again.

resource anything that can be useful.

waste anything discarded as garbage because it is not needed or wanted. It includes dirty liquids from cleaning processes, and gases produced by burning fuels in engines, power plants and industries.

INDEX

Photographic Credits:
Cover and pages 10, 13, 15, 20 and 34: Frank Spooner Pictures; page 2-3: Spectrum Colour Library; page 4-5: Planet Earth Pictures; pages 6-7 and 23: Network Photographers; pages 8-9, 11, 12-13 and 24: The Environmental Picture Library; pages 14 and 28-29: Robert Harding Picture Library; page 18-19: Greenpeace; pages 21, 22, 25 and 33: Topham Picture Source; page 29: Science Photo Library; pages 30, 31 and 32: Hutchison Library.